Life·size
Baby Animals

Chirpy chimp

Baby chimpanzees are mischievous and full of fun. They are also very intelligent. Young chimps learn to pick up sticks to collect insects to eat, a little like you use a spoon or fork to eat food. They stay with their mum until they are about seven years old.

Mum and Baby

I am about 80 cm (31 in) tall.

I am about 40 cm (16 in) tall.

Play time
Baby chimps play with their mother and each other. They enjoy swinging through the trees and climbing up trunks. They love to ride on their mum's back, grasping onto her fur.

Sleep soundly
Each night, high up in the trees, chimpanzees make fresh nests from leaves and twigs to sleep in.

Hello!
I like you...

Chimp Tales

- Chimps live together in big groups, called communities.

- A baby chimp has a pink face, which turns darker as it grows older.

- Chimpanzees are our closest living relatives.

3

Cuddly rabbits

A newborn baby rabbit has no fur, but within a few days it grows a soft, furry coat. As babies, they feed on their mother's milk. Because the milk is so rich, they only need to feed for a few minutes twice a day.

I want to hop over the page and explore!

Mum and Baby

I am about 40 cm (16 in) long.

I am about 20 cm (8 in) long.

Nesting

Most baby rabbits stay in nests underground until they are about three weeks old. They are then ready to leave the nest and explore. Many rabbits live together in underground burrows, called warrens.

Munching

When baby rabbits are about three to four weeks old they are ready to munch on grass, plants, and leaves. They might even escape into a vegetable patch!

We are four weeks old.

Baby crocodile

A mother crocodile watches over her babies as they begin to swim in the water, guarding them from any animals that might attack. The baby shown here is a Philippine Crocodile – he will stay with his mum till he is about two years old.

Crocodile Tales

- A nest of crocodile eggs is called a clutch.

- Crocodile babies are called hatchlings.

- Some adult crocodiles can eat animals as big as zebras or deer.

- Crocodiles live for about eighty years.

Watch out ... I can SNAP!

Breaking out

The mother digs a small hole in which she lays her eggs, and then covers them with sand. When the babies are ready to hatch, they start to chirp. Their mum cracks the shells gently in her mouth to help them break free.

I am 18 months old.

Carrying baby

A mother crocodile is very protective of her newborn babies. She tenderly carries them in her mouth, taking them to a safe part of the river. Here they feed on insects and tiny fish.

Mum and Baby

I am about 2 m (6½ ft) long.

I am about 46 cm (18 in) long.

Curious kittens

Young kittens are full of fun and keen to explore and play. They love to chase toys and pounce on string, and play fight, too. This is how they learn to hunt and fight for real when they are fully grown.

Carry kitten

Kittens purr if they're contented, and they will meow if frightened. If the mother thinks a kitten is in danger, she will carry it gently by the scruff of its neck to a safer place.

Cat Tales

- Kittens are born blind.

- A cat recognizes her kittens by their smell.

- A male cat is called a tom and a female is called a molly or queen.

- Cats have great night vision. They need only one-sixth of the amount of light we need.

Let's play all day!

Keeping clean

Cats and kittens spend a lot of time licking their coats to keep them clean. They lick each other's coats as well as their own.

We are one month old.

Mum and Baby

I am about 46 cm (18 in) long.

I am about 15 cm (6 in) long.

Little foal

Foals are usually born in the spring, when the weather is warm and the grass is green and lush, and just right for eating. The mother usually gives birth to a single foal at night time, keeping well away from any possible danger.

Wobbly start

A newborn foal gets up on her wobbly legs within an hour of being born. After only one day, the foal is ready to run with the rest of the herd.

Pony Tales

- A pony is a type of small horse.

- A foal is a pony or horse under one year old.

- A horse or pony can sleep standing up.

- Horses and ponies are measured in units called hands. A hand equals 10.16 cm (4 in).

Hello! I'm so tall...

Mum and Baby

I am a pony and am about 14 hands (147 cm/58 in) tall.

I am about 7 hands (71 cm/28 in) tall.

Munching grass

With their long legs, foals can find it difficult to reach down and feed on grass. A foal's legs are almost the same length as they will be when she is fully grown.

I am two weeks old.

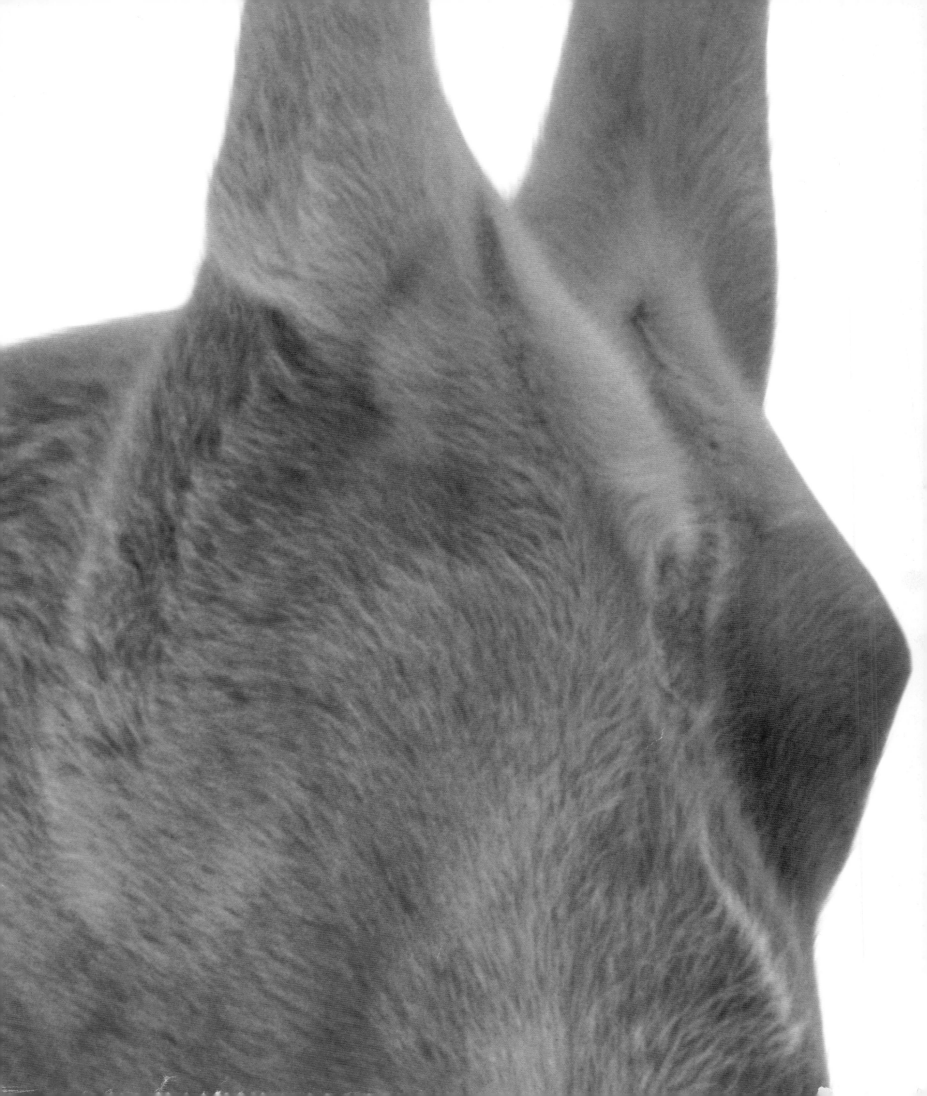

...my legs are nearly as long as Mum's!

Fluffy ducklings

A mother duck builds a nest from leaves and small sticks near a pond or river and lines it with her own soft feathers. She lays about eight eggs and sits on them to keep them warm. About a month later, the ducklings begin to hatch. They follow the first creature they see – their mother.

Chip, chip
A duckling has a special tooth called an egg tooth on the tip of its beak. It uses this to chip through its shell. Once the duckling has hatched, the egg tooth falls off.

Duck Tales

- A male duck is called a drake and is more brightly coloured than a female duck.

- An adult duck's outer feathers are covered with oil to keep them waterproof.

- A duck's webbed feet help it to paddle fast in the water.

- To go to sleep, a duck turns its head backwards and buries its beak in its feathers.

We are two weeks old.

Follow the leader

A mother duck leads her ducklings to a pond or river
about a day after they have hatched. The ducklings stay
close to their mother at first, but in just a few weeks they
will be ready to swim on their own.

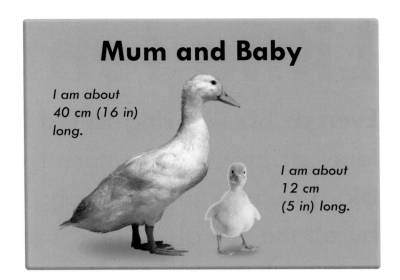

Mum and Baby

I am about
40 cm (16 in)
long.

I am about
12 cm
(5 in) long.

Come on, keep up!

Little lemur

Even as babies, ring-tailed lemurs have long, stripey tails. Lemurs live together in big groups and their young are cared for by all the females. Lemurs spend a lot of time on the ground, but are good at climbing trees, too.

I am six weeks old.

Mum! Mum!

Piggy back
Baby lemurs love to ride on their mother's back, clinging tightly. From only three weeks old, they are ready to start climbing trees.

Watch me climb!

Mum and Baby

I am only about 20 cm (8 in) long... but just look at my tail!

I am about 40 cm (16 in) long, and my tail is even longer.

Sun worshippers

In the morning, ring-tailed lemurs like to sit together and sunbathe. They sit facing the sun, with their legs and arms spread out wide. This helps them stay warm all day.

Lemur Tales

- Lemurs sometimes huddle in a group, called a lemur ball.

- They wave their smelly tails in the air to warn rivals to stay away.

- Lemurs are noisy — they purr, grunt, and howl to each other.

- Lemurs are only found on the African island of Madagascar.

Lion cub

Baby lions are called lion cubs. They live with their mother and father in a group of lions, called a pride. Lion cubs love to play – just like you do! All the female lions in a pride help look after the cubs, until they are fully grown.

Feeding
A lioness gives birth to up to six cubs at a time, and feeds them on her milk. After about eight weeks, the cubs are ready to join the other lions in the pride.

Can we play chase now?

Play time
Little lion cubs are very playful. They especially like chase and wrestling games. They love to climb over Mum – and sometimes Dad, if they get the chance!

Mum and Baby

I am about 107 cm (42 in) tall.

I am about 25 cm (10 in) tall.

Lion Tales

- Female lions do most of the hunting.

- Male lions have big, hairy manes.

- Adult lions spend most of the day sleeping and resting.

I am six weeks old.

17

Baby seal

A Harp Seal gives birth to her baby, called a pup, on ice. The mother can tell her pup apart from other baby seals just by his smell. Once the pup has grown up he spends most of his time swimming through chilly waters beneath the ice.

I am newborn.

Mother's milk

Seals give birth to one pup at a time. The pup feeds on his mother's milk for about two weeks — but in that time he grows quickly, because the milk is so rich.

Learning to swim

After two weeks, the pup is left to fend for himself. He learns to dive and swim through the water and to hunt for fish. As he grows, his white coat turns grey.

Mum and Baby

I am pretty big — about 2 m (6 ft) long.

I am about half Mum's size, so 1 m (3 ft) long.

Seal Tales

- Harp Seals can stay under water for up to 15 minutes at a time.

- A Harp Seal is born with a fluffy white-yellow coat, which turns pure white after a few days.

- Harp Seals dive to depths of about 100 m (328 ft).

- A Harp Seal's eyes are pure black.

I want to swim, splash, and dive in the water!

Little llama

Most llamas live in herds in the mountains of Peru in South America. Llamas are very friendly and clever animals. Adult llamas look out for their young and care for each other. If they hear a noise or feel under threat, they send out a loud warning noise.

Family life
A baby llama is usually born with all the female llamas gathered around him for protection. Baby llamas can stand up and walk about an hour after birth.

Mum and Baby

I am about 107 cm (42 in) tall.

I am about 72 cm (28 in) tall.

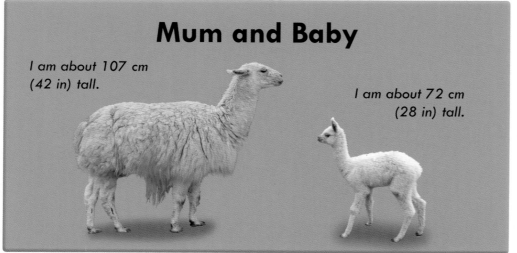

Climbing high
Llamas are great climbers. They have pads on the bottom of their feet which give them good grip on high mountain sides. Young llamas soon learn to climb as well as their parents.

I am one week old.

My coat is really cosy!

Playful puppy

Newborn puppies are tiny and helpless. But once they start feeding they soon begin to grow and are ready to play! The puppy shown here is a Border Collie. These dogs are lively and intelligent, and make great sheep dogs.

Dog Tales

- The tallest dog breed on average is the Irish Wolfhound at about 79 cm (31 in) tall.

- The smallest breed is the Chihuahua at about 15–23 cm (6–9 in) in height.

- Dalmatian puppies are born without any black spots.

Puppy love

When puppies are first born they are blind, deaf, and totally dependent on their mum. The babies feed on their mother's milk for about a month until they are ready to eat solid food.

Great! I love this game – you throw the ball!

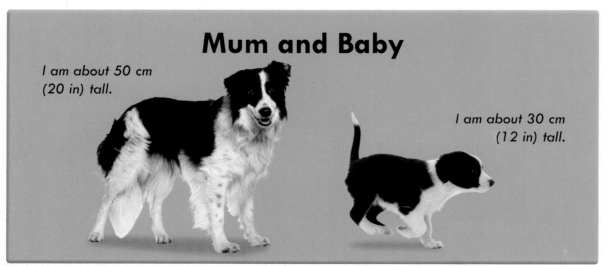

Mum and Baby

I am about 50 cm (20 in) tall.

I am about 30 cm (12 in) tall.

I'm six weeks old.

Puppy play

Puppies love to play wrestling and chase games. They even bite each other — but only playfully, not to cause hurt. They also learn to wag their tails to signal to each other and to show they're happy!

Can we play again?

Fluffy penguin

A penguin chick is covered in thick, fluffy down. She sometimes nestles on Mum or Dad's feet to keep warm. The penguins shown here are Emperor Penguins. Many live in a cold, icy area called Antarctica.

Egg warmer
The mother penguin lays one egg, then journeys out to sea to hunt for fish. Dad stays behind, keeping the egg warm on top of his feet. Around the time the egg hatches, Mum returns to look after her chick.

Huddled together
Penguin chicks huddle together to keep warm while their parents go hunting for fish in the frozen seas. They take it in turns to stand in the middle of the group, where it's warmest.

Mum and Baby
I am about 1.2 m (4 ft) tall.

I am about 35 cm (14 in) tall.

I've found a cosy spot!

I am five weeks old.

Penguin Tales

- Penguins are birds, but they cannot fly.

- Penguins are great swimmers, but they can only waddle on land.

- The Emperor Penguin is the largest type of penguin.

- The Little Blue Penguin, or Fairy Penguin, is the smallest at about 40 cm (16 in) tall.

Little goat

Goats are clever, curious, and friendly animals. When only a few weeks old, baby goats, called kids, are ready to explore their surroundings. Naturally quick and agile, kids soon learn to follow their mother and climb up the steepest, rockiest mountains.

Mother love
Mother goats often give birth to twins. The kids feed from their mother's milk and stay close to her at all times. Even when they're older, they prefer to stay close to Mum.

I fancy a nibble!

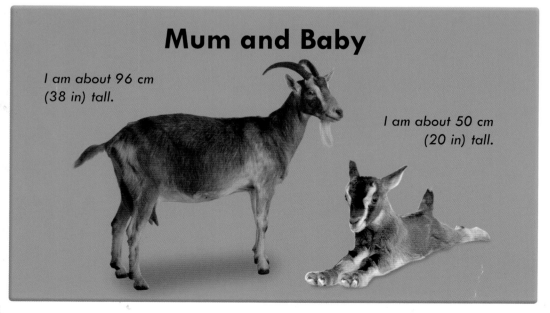

Mum and Baby

I am about 96 cm (38 in) tall.

I am about 50 cm (20 in) tall.

Great climbers

Kids soon learn to climb, run, and jump up high. They can even climb over fences. They can stand on their back legs to reach tree branches and shrubs to feed.

I am three weeks old.

Goat Tales

- When goats give birth it's called "kidding".

- A male goat is a buck or billy; a female is a doe or nanny.

- Goats are so good at climbing, they can even climb up into trees.

Wide-eyed owlets

Baby owls are called owlets. When they first hatch, owlets are covered in fluffy white down. Owls do not build their own nests, they look for abandoned nests in trees, in underground burrows or in barns and caves.

Hatching

Mother owl lays three to five white, round eggs. After about one month, the owlets hatch. But they do not hatch at the same time — this is why baby owlets differ in size.

Look over there! I spy a mouse...

Daddy owl

Owlets are cared for by both Mum and Dad. While Mum goes off hunting for food, Dad stays in the nest and cares for the little ones.

We are one month old.

Mum and Baby

I am about 23 cm (9 in) tall.

I am about 15 cm (6 in) tall, though my fluffy feathers make me look even bigger!

29

Glossary

Here are some words and their meanings that you may find helpful when learning about animal babies.

Bonding A parent and baby growing emotionally closer to each other.

Burrow A hole or tunnel under the earth where animals, such as rabbits, live.

Camouflage An animal's colour or markings that help it to blend into its surroundings.

Develop To grow and change naturally.

Down Fine, soft feathers that cover a baby bird.

Grooming When an animal cleans its fur or cleans another animal's fur.

Hand A unit of measurement, which equals 10.16 cm (4 in), used to measure the height of a horse. Traditionally, it was the width of an adult human hand.

Snap! Snap!

Hatching When an animal emerges out of its shell.

Herd Animals of one kind that live together as a group.

Intelligence The ability to learn, use knowledge, and think about things.

Mammal A warm-blooded animal that is covered in fur or hair, breathes with lungs, and feeds its young on milk.

Mating When a male and female animal come together to make babies.

Nest A home built by animals, especially birds, for laying eggs and for bringing up their young.

Owlet A small or young owl.

Pony A type of small horse under 14.2 hands in height.

Predator An animal that hunts another animal in order to kill and eat it.

Prey An animal that is killed and eaten by another animal.

Pride A group of lions that live together.

Relatives Members of a family group, such as brothers and sisters, mothers and fathers, uncles and aunts.

Reptile A cold-blooded animal that has a dry, scaly, and waterproof skin.

Webbed Thin pieces of skin joining the toes of an animal, especially birds.

A note on sizes

Animal sizes vary enormously. The sizes given in this book are based on average sizes for the type of animal shown, within a few centimetres or inches.

DK

LONDON, NEW YORK, MUNICH,
MELBOURNE and DELHI

Written by Marie Greenwood
Designed by Polly Appleton
Illustrations by Jenna Riggs
Picture research Polly Appleton
Consultant Kim Dennis-Bryan Ph.D, FZS
Design development manager Helen Senior
Publishing manager Bridget Giles
Category publisher Sue Leonard
Production Jen Lockwood
Production editor Andy Hilliard

First published in Great Britain in 2012 by
Dorling Kindersley Limited,
80 Strand, London WC2R 0RL
A Penguin Company
2 4 6 8 10 9 7 5 3 1
182844 – 5/12
Copyright © 2012 Dorling Kindersley Limited, London.

Goodbye everyone!

Picture credits

The publisher would like to thank the following for their kind
permission to reproduce their photographs:
(Key: a-above; b-below/bottom; c-centre; f-far; l-left; r-right; t-top)

Corbis: Dan Guravich 18bl; Peter Guttman 20bc; Frans Lanting 24. **Dorling Kindersley:**
Barrie Watts 13tr, 13cl, 32. **Dreamstime.com:** Isselee 1bl, 1br, 8, 9bl, 9br, 9l, 16bc, 16-17,
22bl, 26bc, 26-27, 29cl, 29cr, 29br; Robert Mawby 21; Vladimir Melnik 18-19, 31. **Fotolia:**
Eric Isselée 14bc, 14-15; Vladimir Melnik 18bc; Peter Wey 7bc. **Getty Images:** National
Geographic / Joel Sartore 6-7, 7br, 30; Robert Harding World Imagery / Thorsten Milse
24-25. **Warren Photographic Limited:** 4b, 4-5, 5tr, 5bl, 5br, 5ftr, 22bc, 22-23.
Jacket images: Front: **Fotolia:** Eric Isselée. Back: **Fotolia:** Eric Isselée cr.
Warren Photographic Limited: bl.

All other images © Dorling Kindersley
For further information see: **www.dkimages.com**